THIS BOOK IS A GIFT TO:

Mrs Mac

MESSAGE:

We Love You!!
Thanks For All
You Do!

FROM:

Mrs Kim

Blessings of Joy

© 2013 Christian Art Gifts, RSA
      Christian Art Gifts Inc., IL, USA

Art © Bethany Berndt-Shackelford, licensed by Suzanne Cruise

Designed by Christian Art Gifts

Printed in China

ISBN 978-1-4321-0733-8

Blessings

of

JOY

MESSAGES

to Delight & Cheer

christian
art gifts ®

REJOICE
ALWAYS
PRAY **WITHOUT CEASING**

give thanks
IN ALL

CIRCUMSTANCES

{1 Thess. 5:16-18}

May your **JOYS** be as deep

as the ocean, your sorrows as

LIGHT as its foam.

ANONYMOUS

JOY runs DEEPER

than despair.

CORRIE ten BOOM

Rejoice
IN THE
LORD
AND BE
GLAD.
{Ps. 32:11}

YOU MAKE ME
GLAD
BY YOUR DEEDS, **Lord;**
I SING FOR

 *joy*

AT THE WORK YOUR
HANDS HAVE
DONE.
[Ps. 92:4]

Those who bring **SUNSHINE**

into the **LIVES** of others,

cannot keep it from themselves.

SIR JAMES M. BARRIE

Let the world see your **JOY** and you won't

be able to keep them away. To be filled

with God is to be **FILLED** with **JOY**.

ANONYMOUS

The

LORD

IS MY

STRENGTH

AND MY

SONG.

[Ps. 118:14]

THE LORD

your **GOD** will bless **YOU**
in all your **HARVEST**

&

in **ALL** the work of your
hands, and your

JOY

WILL BE COMPLETE.

{Deut. 16:15}

Keep the **JOY** of loving God in your

heart and **SHARE** this joy

with all you meet.

MOTHER TERESA

YOU **SHALL** go out in *joy* and be led forth in PEACE

Isa. 55:12

The surest mark of a Christian is

not **FAITH,** or even **LOVE,** but **JOY.**

SAMUEL M. SHOEMAKER

HAPPY is the person who not only sings,

but feels God's eye is on the sparrow,

and knows He **WATCHES** over me. To be

simply ensconced in God is **TRUE JOY**.

ALFRED A. MONTAPERT

IN HIM

our **HEARTS**

rejoice,

for we **TRUST** in His

**HOLY
NAME**

{Ps. 33:21}

LET THE

hearts

of those who

SEEK

the Lord

rejoice.

[Ps. 105:3]

It is His **JOY** that remains in us

that makes our **JOY FULL.**

A. B. SIMPSON

There is no **JOY** in the world

like the joy of bringing

one **SOUL** to **CHRIST.**

WILLIAM BARCLAY

SING
& make music

in your **HEART** to
THE LORD.

[EPH. 5:19]

THOSE WHO
SOW
in tears **WILL**
REAP

with songs

of joy.

[Ps. 126:5]

When our **LIVES** are filled with

PEACE, FAITH and **JOY,** people

will want to know what we have.

Dᴀᴠɪᴅ Jᴇʀᴇᴍɪᴀʜ

Oɴᴇ ᴊᴏʏ scatters

a hundred griefs.

Pʀᴏᴠᴇʀʙ

The joy of the **LORD** is your **STRENGTH.**

{Neh. 8:10}

JOY is the **HOLY FIRE** that keeps our purpose **WARM** and our intelligence **AGLOW.**

HELEN KELLER

I WILL **REJOICE** in the **LORD!** I will be *joyful* in the God of my **SALVATION**

{Hab. 3:18}

The **PUREST** joy in the world

is **JOY** in Christ Jesus.

ROBERT MURRAY M'CHEYNE

In this world, full often, our **JOYS**

are only the **TENDER** shadows

which our sorrows cast.

Henry Ward Beecher

LET ALL WHO TAKE

REFUGE

in **YOU** rejoice;
let them ever
SING for joy.

[Ps. 5:11]

Worship

the Lord with

GLADNESS;

come before **Him**
with joyful

SONGS.

{Ps. 100:2}

JOY is the experience of knowing
that you are unconditionally LOVED.

HENRI NOUWEN

Occasionally in **LIFE** there are

those moments of unutterable

FULFILLMENT which

cannot be completely explained

by those symbols called words.

Their **MEANINGS** can only

be articulated by the inaudible

language of the **HEART.**

MARTIN LUTHER KING, JR.

You **fill** me with

JOY

in **Your**

presence.

{Ps. 16:11}

BE HAPPY!

Yes, leap for *joy*!
For a great
reward awaits
YOU
in **heaven**.

[Luke 6:23]

JOY is not necessarily the absence of suffering, it is the PRESENCE of God.

SAM STORMS

Delight

yourself in the Lord,
and *He will* give you

∽ THE ∽

DESIRES

of your *heart.*

{Ps. 37:4}

Seek **JOY** in what you

GIVE, not in what you get.

ANONYMOUS

JOY is a net of **LOVE** by which you

can catch souls. A joyful heart is

the inevitable result of a **HEART**

burning with **LOVE.**

MOTHER TERESA

THOSE WHO

look to Him

for help **will** be
radiant with

JOY

no shadow of shame

━━━━ ◆►─ will ─◄◆ ━━━━

DARKEN

their faces.

{Ps. 34:5}

There is a **JOY** which

is not given to the ungodly, but to

those who **LOVE** Thee for Thine own sake,

whose joy Thou Thyself art. And this is the

HAPPY LIFE, to **REJOICE**

to Thee, of Thee, for Thee; this it is,

and there is **NO OTHER.**

ST. AUGUSTINE

He who goes out weeping,
bearing
the seed for
SOWING

shall come home
with **shouts** of
joy

{Ps. 126:6}

BE TRULY GLAD.

There is **wonderful** joy

ahead,

even though you have to

endure many trials for

a little while.

[1 Pet. 1:6]

Everyone knows how to **SMILE.**
It's one of the greatest **GIFTS** God has
given us. A smile makes people feel **GOOD,**
and people look so **BEAUTIFUL** when
they smile. When the **JOY** in your life is
obvious, it **RUBS OFF** on others.

Joyce Meyer

In **Him** our hearts

REJOICE

for we
trust in **HIS**

holy name.

May Your unfailing **love** be with us
LORD, even as we put our **hope** in

You.

{Ps. 33:21-22}

Be joyful.

Grow to maturity.
Encourage each other.

Live in

HARMONY
&
PEACE.

Then the God of **love**
and **peace** will be with
you.

(2 Cor. 13:11)

JOY has its springs deep DOWN inside.
And that spring never runs dry, no matter
what happens. Only JESUS gives that joy.
He had joy, singing its music within, even
under the shadow of the CROSS.

S. D. GORDON

No **one** can get

joy

by **merely** asking for it.

It is one of the ripest

FRUITS

of the Christian life, and
like all **fruits,** must be

grown.

HENRY DRUMMOND